WHICH CROSS
are YOU?

Britton Ferrell

authorHOUSE·

AuthorHouse™
1663 Liberty Drive
Bloomington, IN 47403
www.authorhouse.com
Phone: 833-262-8899

Published by AuthorHouse 04/18/2023

ISBN: 979-8-8230-0649-1 (sc)
ISBN: 979-8-8230-0648-4 (e)

Library of Congress Control Number: 2023907350

Print information available on the last page.

Contents

In the beginning, God created the heavens and the earth. The earth was without form and void, and darkness was on the face of the deep. And the Spirit of God was hovering over the face of the waters.

—Genesis 1:1–2

In the beginning, was the Word and the
Word was with God, and the Word was God.
He was in the beginning with God.

—John 1:1–2

Holy, Holy, Holy God in three persons is blessed Trinity. In the beginning and still today, God exists in three persons: God the Father; God the Son, Jesus, our Holy Savior; and God the Holy Spirit, our friend and helper. According to scripture, these three have always been from the beginning. This message will concentrate on a time when all three were together, interceding for our souls and bridging the gap between sin and God's love for us. A time when Jesus's faith, bolstered by God's Spirit, made it possible to receive God's grace born through blood, nails, thorns, and a cross.

The day of redemption marked by three crosses should represent some part of our life. Somewhere in our life, we have been on one side of Jesus or the other. Somewhere in our life, we have been the thief on the left who ridiculed, cursed, and never accepted our circumstances. Or we have been the thief on the right who realized how foolish it is to try to handle our shortcomings and challenges when our Savior is in the middle, offering to make paradise available. Which cross are you?

The Crosses and the Trinity

The three crosses also represent our relationship with the Trinity. The left cross represents rejection and the individual criticizing Christ, while on the cross represents our sinful nature. The cross in the middle represents salvation, our Lord and Savior, Jesus Christ, who made our sinful nature forgiven and replaced by God the Father's unfailing grace. The right cross represents redemption, our redeemed nature, as shown by the thief's willingness to admit his guilt, recognize it, and then repent asking for Jesus, who was hanging on the cross just like him, to forgive him. The thief acknowledged our Lord and Savior, asked for forgiveness, and was promised eternity in paradise. The second thief turned from his sinful nature and confessed, allowing God's grace through the sacrifice of His Son, our Lord, to pour out in the form of forgiveness.

The cross is the meeting point between us and Jesus, God the Father Almighty, and the Holy Spirit, our Helper and our Friend. It bridges the gap between us and sin so that we may have an everlasting relationship with Jesus and through Jesus. On the cross, the sinful thief met Jesus and came to receive God's grace poured out through Jesus on the cross. So we, as the thief, can also meet Jesus, turn from our sins, and receive all of God's grace, mercy, and blessings made possible through the cross and His Son, our Lord Jesus Christ.

Britton Ferrell

Focus through the Storm

Draw near to God, and He will draw near
to you. Cleanse your hands, you sinners, and
purify your hearts, you double-minded.

—James 4:8

Lord, if it's you, tell me to come to you on the water.
Come, He said. Then Peter got down out of the
boat, walked on the water, and came toward Jesus.
But when he saw the wind and the waves, he was
afraid and, beginning to sink, cried out, Lord save
me! Immediately Jesus reached out His hand and
caught him. You of little faith, why did you doubt?

—Matthew 14:28–31

Britton Ferrell

Countless distractions in the Christian life threaten to derail and distract us from our life with God. Our lives are constantly full of "noise," such as cell phones, bills, loss of loved ones, quotas, long commutes, long hours at work, annoying neighbors, annoying coworkers, etc. This is by design because the devil would love nothing better, and his goal is to distract us from our Savior. If we are distracted, we lose our focus, which is supposed to be on God, Jesus, and listening to the Holy Spirit.

Dear friends, do not waste your time on pointless debates and endless rabbit trails that steal you from the lived experience of the Spirit of God. Instead, one can have excellent knowledge about the Christian faith and even engage others in the name of Christ, arguing for positions and beliefs that are worthy of praise and defense yet entirely missing the point.

God is waiting for you. He longs to know you and be known by you. Therefore, do not waste your life on empty pursuits. Do not fill your days with religious noise or busyness that fills your head and empties your heart. Instead, draw near so that He may draw near to you. In the example of Peter, we see several things illustrated. Jesus called for Peter to come closer, and Peter, out of obedience, stepped out of the boat on faith and went toward Jesus. Second, the Bible tells us Peter was walking on water until he got distracted by the waves, the wind, and everything the storm brought with it. When Peter focused on Jesus, he did not sink, but when he focused on the reality of the storm, not on Jesus, he began to sink. Thirdly, the Bible tells us that as Peter started to sink, he cried out to Jesus, and Jesus immediately reached

Britton Ferrell

out and caught him. This tells us that Jesus is always focused on us as well.

One example in my own life to share involves a bill coming due and no money to pay for it. I was failing at my job and hadn't paid myself in ten years. My spouse was the breadwinner and the sole means of income into our household. Time and circumstances had finally caught up with me to the point where I couldn't fake success anymore. The bill was coming due and I had nowhere to hide and no excuses. There we sat, the two of us in our kitchen, with the bill in one hand and questions of how we would make this work in the other. I, like Peter, focused on the storm and the waves. My spouse, on the other hand, had unwavering faith and said we'd be OK. Two weeks later a check came in the mail. The bill due was from one company, but the check that came was from a completely different company and equaled the bill due—to the penny. I sat there in tearful amazement while my spouse sat there in tearful fulfillment. I share that story to bolster your faith that we never know when and where God's love will come to fulfillment in our lives. We have to walk by faith so that His eye is always on us and His love is always available and ready for us to ask for and receive.

The disciples knew their journey with Jesus had the potential for storms and surprises. Yet when that potential became a reality, their faith crumbled. Faith is the unwavering trust in the mercy and goodness of God regardless of situation or circumstance. There is never a moment in which you cannot trust God, no matter how desperate or dire your situation may be, whether at the kitchen table or even at the cross.

Just as the thief was being nailed to the cross, I'm sure he could not help but be surrounded by his situation. The Roman guards, the cross, the nails being hammered into his hands and feet, the sound of people crying and jeering. It wasn't until his focus changed that he saw and realized the Savior he had in Jesus. But just like the noises and storms we experience daily, the thief reset his focus and found Jesus. He reset his focus and found redemption, so we can also reset our focus and find our Savior and redemption.

Humility and Repentance

And Peter remembered the saying of Jesus. Before the rooster crows, you will deny me three times. And he went out and wept bitterly. When morning came, all the chief priests and the elders of the people took counsel against Jesus to put him to death. And they bound him, led him away, and delivered him to Pilate, the governor. Then when Judas, his betrayer, saw that Jesus was condemned, he changed his mind and returned the thirty pieces of silver to the chief priests and the elders, saying, I have sinned by betraying innocent blood. They said, What is that to us? See to it yourself.

—Matthew 26:75; 27:1–4

To sin is to be human, yet how we respond to our sin defines the type of lives we live and the people we are becoming. In quick succession, the Gospel of Matthew presents a snapshot of two men suffering under the weight of sin and self-made alienation at their worst. One is ashamed of his fear and unwilling to identify with Christ during his trial. The other is broken by his betrayal of the man he had promised to follow and honor as Lord. Peter and Judas suffer from the same sickness in many ways, yet their response to their ailment sets them apart.

Though closely related, there is a profound difference between remorse and repentance. All genuine repentance begins with remorse, yet remorse does not always lead to repentance. Please pay attention to this truth, for it is a key to our growth in the spiritual life. Many people are blind to their sin, unaware of how their words and actions cause harm to those around them. Or, even worse, they see this harm yet are so self-absorbed that they are indifferent to the suffering of others and care only for themselves and their advancement. As such, we must pray for our eyes to see our sin and that God would grant us sorrow over it. This Godly sorrow is the heart of remorse, seeing and regretting one's actions with the awareness of the harm they bring to others and ourselves.

When in a place of remorse, we have two paths that lie before us. Sorrow without any hope for the future or sorrow rooted in the belief that the Lord can bind our wounds and bring life where there is only death. This second path is the way of repentance, a path that Peter alone chose to walk. As he began to realize the depth of his deception and disease, Judas was deeply remorseful, yes, but failed to believe there was any possibility for the healing of so great a wound. Judas, therefore, walked his chosen path to its inevitable end, one of self-made destruction. On the other hand, Peter wept bitterly over his shortcomings, choosing to remain close to Christ, turning toward him again and again, and it was in this nearness Peter's healing was found. Peter did not heal himself, but in choosing to stay near Jesus, he placed himself in the river from which healing waters flow. This is the invitation that lies before us as well. No matter how desperate or dire your situation may be, can you return to Jesus and stay close to him, inviting him to make all things new, even your own life?

The cross humbles us in order to be exulted in Jesus. The cross is a point of death to sin and a birth to righteousness through the grace given for the forgiveness of those sins through the sacrifice of Jesus. The cross and Jesus are the gateways to heaven and the keys opening the door to God's goodness. It was on the cross that the thief repented of his sins before Jesus and on the cross by which Jesus forgave the thief of his sins. For us to seek and receive forgiveness, reconciliation, and redemption, we need to embrace the cross. But which cross? The cross of Jesus gives us the power to forgive others and exalts us with God's forgiveness.

The Gospel and the Cross

I thank Christ Jesus our Lord, who has given me strength and considered me trustworthy, appointing me to His service. Even though I was once a blasphemer, a persecutor, and a violent man, I was shown mercy because I acted in ignorance and unbelief. The grace of our Lord was poured out on me abundantly, along with the faith and love that are in Christ Jesus. Here is a trustworthy saying that deserves full acceptance: Christ Jesus came into the world to save sinners of whom I am the worst. But for that very reason, I was shown mercy so that in me, the worst of sinners, Christ Jesus, might display his immense patience as an example for those who believe in him and receive eternal life. Now to the King eternal, immortal, invisible, the only God, be honor and glory forever and ever. Amen.

—1 Timothy 1:12–17

We have all at some time experienced anxiousness or some type of trepidation. A college exam, a medical test or procedure, or a business interview—things we need reassurance on due to not knowing the outcome. Jesus experienced these emotions, too, in the Garden of Gethsemane.

> Jesus told his disciples, "My soul is very sorrowful, even to death. Going a little farther He fell on His face and prayed, My Father if it be possible, let this cup pass from me; nevertheless, not as I will, but as you will." (Matthew 26:38–39)

Jesus is our Lord and Savior, but he also experienced human emotions and tribulations. Jesus never sinned and handled them with God's grace and the Holy Spirit's guidance. Jesus prayed and followed God's will, even to the cross.

The gospel and the cross of Jesus are inseparable. The two are forever intertwined as one. They summarize the saving and redemptive mission of Jesus Christ. It is through the cross and, more importantly, through Jesus that God reconciled with us. We all have gone through trials and tribulations— times of loss, suffering, and uncertainty. Nobody who lives long enough cannot go through something, regardless of whether they are a Christian or a nonbeliever. Jesus suffered unto death on the cross to be the perfect example for us so our sins may be forgiven. The cross means letting go of our comfort, but it also means letting go of our uncertainties.

Britton Ferrell

Imagine the thief hanging there sure of where he had come from and sure of certain death but unsure of where his soul would be.

How does the thief on the cross fit into your theology? No baptism, no communion, no confirmation, no speaking in tongues, no mission trips, no volunteerism, and no church clothes. He couldn't even bend his knees to pray. He didn't say the sinner's prayer; among other things, he was a thief. Jesus didn't take away his pain, heal his body, or smite the scoffers. Yet a thief walked into heaven at the same hour as Jesus simply by believing. He had nothing more to offer than believing Jesus was who he said he was. No spin from brilliant theologians. No ego or arrogance. No shiny lights, skinny jeans, or crafty words. No haze machine, doughnuts, or coffee at the entrance. Just a naked dying man on a cross, unable to even fold his hands to pray.

> For the word of the Cross is folly to those who
> are perishing, but to us who are being saved it
> is the power of God. (1 Corinthians 1:18)

Paul's Vision of Paradise

It is doubtless not profitable for me to boast. I will come to visions and revelations of the Lord. I know a man in Christ, who fourteen years ago, whether in the body I do not know, or whether out of the body I do not know, God knows, such a one was caught up to the third Heaven. And I know such a man, whether in the body or out of the body, I do not know, but God knows how he was caught up into Paradise and heard inexpressible words, which it is not lawful for a man to utter. Of such a one I will boast, yet of myself, I will not boast.

—2 Corinthians 12:1:5

God is waiting for you to die to self. The thief realized, hanging on the cross, that it had all come down to that moment, and the only people involved were he and Jesus. In that moment, he had a choice. In that moment, he realized he had only relied on himself all his life. In that moment on the cross, he had a choice. He looked over and saw himself in the other thief, who was hanging there, still hanging on to himself. The thief who would see himself and, in that moment, made a choice even in his final hour to turn from himself and ask Jesus for forgiveness. He placed his belief in Jesus and asked for forgiveness. But in actuality, he also asked Jesus to take his place, which Jesus was actually doing at the time. Even in the final hour, God poured His grace out through His Son Jesus to a thief. A thief who realized his whole life had no real, sustainable purpose. A thief who turned from self to Jesus and gained a whole new purpose in Jesus in paradise. Even as Jesus was taking on our sins and God was turning from Him, Jesus turned to the thief and interceded on his behalf. Even as the thief, in his last moments, realized he had nowhere else to turn, he put his faith in Jesus, maybe and probably out of desperation. But even in those last hours, it counted.

Back to the Cross

It is never too late to return to the cross and Jesus. Even as believers, we all need to return to the cross and Jesus to find ourselves and help others find salvation. The only parts of our salvation Satan can never touch or claim authority over are those parts we have turned over to Jesus. Anything Jesus and the Holy Spirit have anointed can never be broken. No authority or principality can have dominion over us as long as we remain in Jesus.

> Toward the end of the crucifixion, the Bible tells us of the Roman soldiers coming to break the bones of the ones on the crosses. When they came to the body of Jesus, they found him to be already dead so they did not break any of His bones. The still alive thieves were not so lucky as the bones in their legs were broken. John 19:31–33 They asked Pilate to order that the legs of the men be broken … The soldiers came and broke the legs of the two men beside Jesus. But when the soldiers came

close to Jesus, they saw that he was already dead. So they did not break his legs.

We, too, can become unbreakable to the devil's ways when we embrace our Lord and Savior, Jesus Christ, and die to self and sin. Even though his legs were broken, the spirit of the thief on the cross was not broken. He had already found Jesus, he had already repented, he had found his one true Savior, and he received his blessing to be in paradise on the promise of the one true King.

I Wonder if He Smiled

Imagine looking back on your life, I mean the totality of it all, and realizing what you had spent your time on didn't contribute to anything. You didn't grow as a person, you certainly weren't a Christian, and you never helped others but instead took advantage of them either by word or deed.

Imagine that one day you finally got caught and it all came crashing to an end. You were incarcerated, judged, and sentenced to hang on a cross as part of the cruelest form of punishment at the time. Nails hammered through both your wrists and one through both your feet on a rough-hewn piece of wood. Completely exposed to the elements, the crowd, and your thoughts. You are not alone though; two other convicts hang on their own crosses next to you. One you recognize from your own life as he has lived a similar life to yours. The other man in the middle you have heard of but have never met in person, but the stories of the man known as Jesus have been told all across Roman territories.

As you hang contemplating the choices that brought you here, you hear your counterpart across from you mocking

Jesus, cursing, and condemning everybody but himself. You realize this is the attitude that got you here in the first place and choose to change.

My father had been diagnosed with Parkinson's disease. Throughout his last years, his mind deteriorated to the point where sometimes he could not control his emotions and his temper would get the better of him. No fault of his own. It was just a condition of Parkinson's. But as his son being in law enforcement, I would have a natural reaction to his outbursts toward his wife, my mother. One day he grabbed her by the arm to the point where it left visible fingerprints. I simply lost my composure and proceeded to give him the riot act about how a man should not put his hands on a woman and threatened jail time, and on and on. Quite simply, I lost my temper.

As I walked thirty feet away, I heard him ask my wife, "Why did he get on to me like that?" Right then and there, I realized I had let my frustrations of knowing my dad was dying, my selfishness of having to make the effort to care for him, and my ignorance of not accepting his disease catch up with me. I had lost my empathy; I had lost my grace and compassion. The realization of how I was personally handling my dad's disease had all come crashing to a reality that I could not ignore anymore. From that day forward, I conscientiously decided to handle things differently and changed the focus and approach to handling situations like that. I share that story to give hope no matter what situation you find yourself in, do not lose your compassion and empathy but stop, take a step back, and reassess your situation and what you can do to improve it.

You choose to change your heart and mindset amid the worst moment of your life, either from despair or repentance. You see Jesus in the middle praying for others, asking God to "forgive them for they know not what they do." You see Jesus in the same situation as you bearing responsibility for your sin, even though he committed no sin himself and should not be sharing in your fate. You decide there and then that no matter how long you have left, you will accept your fate, ask for forgiveness, and put your faith in Jesus. And then, among all the pain and tears, you receive forgiveness. You receive grace from the One who knew no sin but bore it for your sake so that you may know the love of His Father our God. You hear the words "Today, you will be with Me in paradise." What joy that must be, what relief that must be to hear those words and to know you are forgiven. The Bible doesn't tell us, but I wonder if the thief on the right smiled. If the King of Kings says you are forgiven and tells you to your face you are going to Heaven, that is something to smile about.

Rejoice in Salvation

Rejoice in the Lord always. I will say it again: Rejoice!
Let your gentleness be evident to all. The Lord is near.
Do not be anxious about anything, but in every situation,
by prayer and petition, with thanksgiving, present your
requests to God. And the peace of God, which transcends
all understanding, will guard your hearts and minds in
Christ Jesus. Finally, brothers and sisters, whatever is true,
noble, proper, pure, lovely, and admirable, if anything
is excellent or praiseworthy, think about such things.
Whatever you have learned, received, heard, or seen in me,
put it into practice. And the God of peace will be with you.

—Philippians 4:4–9

The dash analogy could be incorporated into the crucifixion scene. The dash is between the birthdate and the death date on our tombstones. In the crucifixion scene, Jesus is between two thieves, one representing salvation and rebirth and the other representing death. So in essence, Jesus would be in the middle, just like the dash on our tombstones. We are born, go through life (the dash), and then die. During our life, what are we supposed to do? Come to know Jesus as our Lord and Savior, repent of our sins, love one another, and make disciples of people, showing them the way to salvation and grace, glorifying God our Father with the help of His Holy Spirit. That should be our dash. Jesus should represent our dash in between the dates of life.

Salvation is not just rescuing from peril but is equally our entry into paradise. True faith works out in the end. Imagine the cross of Christ as a bridge between Heaven and earth, God and humanity. The life, death, and resurrection of Jesus Christ became a mediator, a go-between, so now all can come to God through total trust in Jesus Christ as the payment for their sins. The severed relationship with perfect love has been restored by perfect love.

Hebrews 12:2 says, "Looking to Jesus, the founder, and perfecter of our faith, who for the joy that was set before Him endured the Cross, despising the shame, and is seated at the right hand of the throne of God."

Imagine, if you will, Jesus in the middle, the unrepenting thief on Jesus's left-hand side, and the repenting thief on Jesus's right-hand side. Jesus sits on God's right side, which means the thief on Jesus's left-hand side represents sin (the rejection cross) having been cleansed, redeemed, and forgiven by Jesus's sacrifice in the middle (the salvation cross). This makes it possible for Jesus to then reach out His left hand to the thief on the right cross (the redemption cross). The blood of Jesus and His sacrifice on the cross made it possible for the thief to find redemption and make it possible for us to receive the same redemption by simply taking Jesus's hand stretched out for us.

If a thief on the cross in his last moments can turn to the Lord and ask for forgiveness and the peace and forgiveness of the Lord our God find him, how much more could we, in our general duties and routines of life, not turn and ask for and find that same peace?

Which cross represents your life? Which cross are you? My hope and prayer are for you to find the salvation cross in the middle, the cross of Jesus, to find and have a relationship with Jesus Christ our Lord and Savior, so that you too will know paradise.

Printed in the United States
by Baker & Taylor Publisher Services